Dealing WITH My Feelings

An Essential Guide to a Child's Well Being & Prosperity

Author

AMEN KAUR

Illustrator

HALEY MOSS

A heartfelt thank you for your purchase.
A percentage of the proceeds will go towards purchasing free books for
underprivileged children.

 FriesenPress

Suite 300 - 990 Fort St
Victoria, BC, V8V 3K2
Canada

www.friesenpress.com

ISBN
978-1-5255-9422-9 (Hardcover)
978-1-5255-9421-2 (Paperback)
978-1-5255-9423-6 (eBook)

1. SELF-HELP, EMOTIONS

Distributed to the trade by The Ingram Book Company

Inspired by my beautiful son (Jodh Singh) and dedicated to all the wonderful children of the world.

How am I Feeling Today?

Happy Playful Curious Proud Peaceful

Sad Lonely Guilty Hurt Embarrassed

Anxious Scared Nervous Worried Left Out

Angry Jealous Annoyed Disrespected Distant

Brave   Shy   Hopeful   Focused   Silly

Bored   Hungry   Sick   Overwhelmed   Tired

Excited   Surprised   Amazed   Shocked   Confused

Apologetic   Cheeky   Creative   Loving   Thankful

Disappointed   Concerned   Relieved   Grief   Grumpy

All feelings are valid. Feelings are just signals that tell our body something is out of balance.

When I feel joyful, confident, content, or inspired . . .

I can . . .

- ⭐ Hug someone I love

- ⭐ Volunteer: share my happiness with others

- ⭐ Do a random act of kindness

- ⭐ Write about it

- ⭐ Dance to my favorite song

- ⭐ Play sports or plan a fun activity

- ⭐ Explore and take pictures of things I love with my camera

- ⭐ Skip rope, go rock climbing, or spend time playing outdoors

- ⭐ Start a new hobby: collect rocks, stamps, cards

- ⭐ Paint and make gratitude rocks or a gratitude bracelet

- ⭐ Build Lego or make a puzzle

- ⭐ Make a gratitude box: celebrate things I am grateful for by writing them down and putting them in the box

- ⭐ Garden or arrange flowers

- ⭐ Use my imagination, get creative and design my own outfit

- ⭐ Do stand up comedy in front of my friends and family

- ⭐ Tell jokes

☆ Play a musical instrument

☆ Fly a kite

☆ Play dress up

☆ Face paint or color in my coloring book

☆ Play Simon says, red light green light, follow the leader, freeze dance, or musical chairs

☆ Make clay pottery

☆ Go for a jog

☆ Watch the sunrise or sunset

When I feel unhappy, isolated, ashamed or remorseful . . .

I can . . .

♫ Tell myself it's normal to feel sad. Everyone feels sad at times.

♪ Sit with my feelings for a few moments.

♩ Close my eyes and notice where I feel sad in my body. Does my chest feel tight? Is my tummy aching?

♫ Cry it out.

♪ Write a letter about it.

♩ List 5 things I love about myself and why.

♫ Remind myself of my past accomplishments and how I overcame them.

♪ Tell myself a positive affirmation. "My heart is safe. I am loved."

♫ Sing about it.

♩ Listen to a sad song.

♪ Watch fish swimming, listen to leaves rustling, birds chirping, or rain falling

♫ Give myself or a stuffed animal a tight hug.

♫ Talk to a caring adult about it.

♩ Spend quality time with a loving adult.

♬ Ask for help.

♪ Spend time with a pet.

♩ Ask someone to make me a warm cup of cocoa.

♬ Draw or paint my sadness.

♪ Move my body, go for a nature walk and notice: what do I see? What can I smell? What sounds do I hear? How do my feet feel from toes to soles?

♩ Put nutritious food in my body.

♬ Ask someone to hold my hand.

♪ Drink my favorite herbal tea.

♩ Smell aromatherapy.

♬ Take a warm bath; pamper myself.

When I feel mad, aggressive, humiliated or withdrawn . . .

I can . . .

- Take 5 deep belly breaths and count each one

- Scribble on paper and then tear it up

- Do 10 jumping jacks

- Scream into a pillow

- Count slowly to 20

- Push against a wall

- Squeeze a stress ball

- Twist a cloth or towel hard like wringing out water until I feel better

- Stomp my feet or pound on clay

- Journal about my feelings

- For every negative thought, write down a positive one

- Imagine a relaxing experience or image that calms me, like being on the beach. What do I hear? Smell? Feel?

- Start an exercise such as running or kickboxing

- Karate chop a cardboard box or take a coloring break

- Listen to music, nature sounds, or sing out loud

- Ask myself if I am hungry or tired
- Watch a funny show or movie
- Squish some putty or pop bubble wrap
- Go to my calm down space
- Do a meditation or repeat a mantra
- Splash some cold water on my face
- Blow bubbles or blow on a pinwheel

When I feel anxious, insecure, helpless or frightened . . .

I can . . .

- Use kind self-talk. I am safe right now.

- Accept it with compassion. It's just a feeling. It will pass.

- Create a worry jar: write down each worry on its own piece of paper. Seal it up tight in a jar to put away and deal with one by one, during a specified later time with a trusted adult. Rip up and throw that worry in the garbage when it no longer needs to be addressed.

- Talk to a trusted family member.

- Empty my mind. Write out all my feelings onto paper.

- Question my thoughts: is my brain playing tricks on me?

- Make a list of things I CAN control.

- Turn off all screens.

- Breathe deep and focus on what is happening right now in the present moment.

- Go swimming or fold laundry.

- Go for a nature hike and pay attention to my surroundings. How does the grass feel in my hands?

- Drink water.

- Clean. Organize. Declutter.

- What five things do I notice? What four things can I touch? What three things can I smell? What one thing can I taste? OR look for my favorite color in the room

- Do my favorite meditation.

- Write down three things I am grateful for.

- Squeeze tight fists, then relax hands. Repeat.

- Stretch or do yoga.

- Listen to the sound of a singing bowl.

- Get more sleep, using a lavender scented diffuser.

- Bake, knead dough by hand, or cook a new recipe.

- Play with Play-Doh, slime, cards, or board games.

- Create a calming glitter jar: Take a jar or bottle, add warm water, glitter glue, food color and glitter. Shake it and watch glitter slowly float to the bottom of the jar.

I can teach my brain to be more positive by adapting a growth mindset. Here's how:

I can . . .

- Always add "yet" to the end of "can't" sentences. For example: I can't figure this out yet.

- Remember that all challenges are opportunities to grow my brain.

- Stretch my brain through learning new things. The more I stretch it, the more intelligent and creative it becomes.

- Always look for ways to improve my "effort." Focus on my own results.

- Seek my own compassion every time, rather than approval from others.

- Ask questions when I don't understand something. Feedback helps me improve.

- Understand that failure means I learn what "doesn't" work so I can do better next time.

- Set small goals to achieve every day.

- Focus on the journey. Learning is magical and my superpower!

- Ask myself: Can this be improved? Is this my best work? If it is, be proud of myself!

- Train my brain to learn anything by trying new things with courage and curiosity.

- Always strive for "progress" not perfection.

- Learn anything I want with hard work and persistence.

- Practice everyday so I can improve and get better. Focus on my strengths.

- Remember that mistakes help me learn better. Embrace them!

- The feeling of things feeling hard is my brain growing.

- Brainstorm possible "solutions" to every problem. Be a problem solver!

- Remember there is always a plan B.

- Know it is always okay to take some time but never give up.

- Tell myself it's okay if some days feel harder than others. I can try again when I am ready.

- Ask myself what new things I can learn everyday.

- Allow the success of others to inspire me.

Respecting and looking after myself will give me high self-esteem. Here are some ways I can feel good about myself:

I can . . .

* Say NO to things I am uncomfortable with.

* Make my own choices and learn from them. Think critically. Every problem can be solved.

* Take care of myself first, body and mind. Meditate, eat well and exercise.

* Refuse to compare myself with others. I am unique.

* Show respect towards myself and others.

* Challenge bad thoughts about myself and replace them with three things I am good at.

* Choose friends who treat me how I want to be treated.

* Think of two qualities I love about myself and write them down every day.

* Practice gratitude everyday and help others.

* Remember that what others say reflects how they feel about themselves.

* Adapt to change. Accepting change helps my body be less stressed.

- ❀ Work on my chores and responsibilities. Doing tasks helps me feel empowered.

- ❀ Look in the mirror and tell myself: "I love you."

- ❀ Complete school assignments and always try new things. Celebrate my accomplishments!

- ❀ Accept myself. No one is perfect. Everyone makes mistakes.

- ❀ Write inspiring messages on paper that encourage me and stick them on my walls or mirror

- ❀ Always speak up. Stand up for what I believe in.

- ❀ Laugh, play, and be silly.

- ❀ Have good posture. Stand tall with shoulders back and chin up!

- ❀ Limit my screen time.

- ❀ Keep visual reminders of things in my room that make me feel good.

- ❀ Do random acts of kindness. Helping others gives me a different perspective.

Guided Meditations

Body-Scan Meditation

- Relax your eyes and forehead
- Unclench your jaw
- Drop your shoulders
- Take a deep belly breath
- Notice how your legs and feet feel
- Pay attention to each area of your body
- Imagine relaxing your body where it feels tense

Balloon Breath Meditation

Step 1: Sit tall or lie on your back and close your eyes

Step 2: Place your hands on your belly, and breathe in and out

Step 3: Notice your belly blow up like a balloon

Step 4: Imagine the balloon deflating as you exhale slowly, letting out the air from your belly

Happy Heart Meditation

1. Sit tall like a mountain, close your eyes, and fold your hands in front of your heart
2. Take a deep breath in and say "thank" in your mind
3. As you breathe out, say "you"
4. Repeat

Grounding Meditation

- Put your hand on your heart and tell yourself "It's okay. This feeling will pass. I will feel happy again."
- Everything you need to heal is already within you. This feeling is not here forever.
- Take a deep breath in and slowly exhale, saying "I am safe. I am loved."

Cocoa Cup Meditation

- Hold a cup of warm cocoa in your hands
- Notice the temperature and how the cup feels in your hands
- Notice the smell and the taste of it in your mouth

Mind Training Meditation

- Pick your favorite object and set it in front of you
- Take three deep breaths as you look at the object
- Notice the colors, shape, texture, and size of it
- When you notice your mind wandering, bring your attention back to the object

5 steps to feeling better

Count 3 things I am grateful for

Meditate

Journal about it

Think: I can self-regulate by...

Start By: naming my feeling

About the Author

Amen Kaur has a BA in psychology and is a certified mindfulness facilitator, born and raised in Canada. She practices mindfulness in her daily life through meditation and creative outlets like writing, designing interiors, or arranging flowers with her son.

Amen Kaur is also the author of Raise Me with Empathy, another book designed to help kids and their parents relate to one another in healthier, more empathetic ways. She is passionate about mindful parenting and runs an Instagram blog page devoted to it.

You can connect with her through her website:
amenkaurbooks.com
where you will also find more information on her blog and books.

About the Illustrator

Haley Moss is a self-taught illustrator (though she likes to think of herself as a professional doodler) based out of Long Island City, New York.

Not just a one-trick pony, Haley's illustration capabilities ranges from cartoons and comics, to graphic design and botanical painting. However, as a lifelong fan of all things Disney and anime, her preferred style is to draw in a big-eyed, colorful way.

Her portfolio can be found at
haleydoods.com

CPSIA information can be obtained
at www.ICGtesting.com
Printed in the USA
BVHW022007181121
621966BV00013B/144